METEORS AND METEORITES
VOYAGERS FROM SPACE

METEORS AND METEORITES
VOYAGERS FROM SPACE

PATRICIA LAUBER

*Illustrated with photographs,
and drawings by Mike Eagle*

SCHOLASTIC INC.
New York Toronto London Auckland Sydney

ISBN 0-590-46409-4

Text copyright © 1989 by Patricia G. Lauber. Illustrations copyright © 1989 by Mike Eagle. All rights reserved. Published by Scholastic Inc., 730 Broadway, New York, NY 10003, by arrangement with Thomas Y. Crowell, an imprint of HarperCollins Publishers.

12 11 10 9 8 7 6 5 4   7 8/9

Printed in the U.S.A.   23

First Scholastic printing, March 1993

Contents

Wethersfield's deputy fire chief examines the hole made by a meteorite that plunged into the Donahues' house.

1.
Raining Rocks?

ON the evening of November 8, 1982, a rock the size of a grapefruit fell out of the sky above Wethersfield, Connecticut. Traveling at three hundred miles an hour, it crashed through the roof of a house, ripped through an upstairs closet, shot into the living room below, bounced sideways into the dining room, hit the ceiling, and finally came to rest under the dining-room table.

The owners of the house, Robert and Wanda Donahue, had been watching television in a room off the kitchen. Their first thought was that they had been bombed. They leaped to their feet, ran through the dining room without seeing the rock, and came to the living room. It was littered with plaster, dust, and bits of wood. The Donahues telephoned for help.

1

Checking the house, firemen discovered the rock. Its outside was a blackened crust, its inside light gray, as a few chipped spots showed. A fireman recognized it for what it was: a meteorite, a rock that had fallen to earth from space.

The Donahue meteorite was about the size of a grapefruit and weighed six pounds.

Meteorites are rare, and it is extremely unusual for them to damage property or injure people or animals. In all of recorded history, only one person is known to have been hurt by a meteorite—a woman in Alabama, who was bruised when a nine-pound meteorite tore through the roof of her house in 1954, bounced off a radio, and hit her. Only fifteen houses are known to have been damaged by meteorites. Oddly enough, two of them were in Wethersfield. In 1971 a meteorite crashed into a house there and lodged in the living-room ceiling.

Stranger yet, the Donahues' meteorite was the third known to have hit the small state of Connecticut. The first fell on December 14, 1807, in the town of Weston.

About 6:30 that morning, while the day was still dark, Nathan Wheeler was walking through a field on his farm in northeastern Weston (now called Easton). A sudden flash lighted up everything around him. Looking up, he saw a ball of fire in the sky to the north. Elihu Staples, who lived nearby, heard three loud noises that sounded like cannon fire and saw the fireball give three leaps. A rushing sound, like a whirlwind, passed to the east of his house, and something heavy hit the ground. On a neighboring farm, terrified cattle jumped a fence, and the farmer later came on a place where the ground was torn up and littered with fragments of unfamiliar rock.

At the time, few people had heard of meteorites, and the farmers of Weston did not know what to make of this strange event—a brilliant light, explosions, and a rain of rocks. But they searched for fallen rocks, hoping these might hold gold or at least have value as souvenirs.

One person who did know about meteorites was Benjamin Silliman, a science professor at Yale College in New Haven. He had learned about them while studying in

France, and when he heard of the fireball, he seized the chance to learn more. Hurrying to Weston, he spent a week interviewing everyone who might have seen the fireball and trying to collect samples of the rock for study. Later, Silliman managed to buy a 25-pound piece for Yale. He estimated that the whole meteorite must have weighed 350 pounds.

The Weston fireball was important because it was the first recorded fall of a meteorite in North America. Silliman's studies were important because they helped to prove that from time to time rocks did fall to earth out of the sky. For hundreds of years learned men had refused to believe that such a thing could happen. They scoffed at reports telling of exploding fireballs and rains of rocks. Not until the late 1700s and early 1800s did some scientists begin to believe that there were rocks in space that sometimes fell to earth. This change of mind opened up a new field of study.

Today we know that there are vast quantities of rocky objects and dust particles in the solar system. They travel around the sun in paths called orbits, just as the planets do. As long as these objects are in space, they are known as meteoroids.

Some meteoroids travel in orbits that cross the earth's orbit. If the earth and a meteoroid happen to meet at a crossing point, the meteoroid plunges into the earth's atmosphere. Traveling as fast as forty-five miles a second, the speeding meteoroid collides with molecules of air and is heated by friction, just as a returning space capsule is.

Meteoroids that glow with heat are called meteors. Most are no bigger than grains of sand. When they are heated, they burn up, or turn to vapor, leaving a trail of brightly glowing gases. They are seen in the night sky as

Meteors look like falling stars, but they are not. These bright streaks of light are caused by dust particles that plunge into the earth's atmosphere and burn up.

streaks of brilliant light that suddenly appear and just as suddenly disappear. Although many people speak of them as falling stars or shooting stars, their correct name is meteors.

Sometimes meteoroids the size of your fist or bigger plunge into the atmosphere. They form the brightest meteors of all and are called fireballs. The brightest fireballs may outshine the moon or even the sun. A fireball has a brilliant, tear-shaped head and is accompanied by a trail of light and scattered sparks.

Meteoroids and meteors that survive their trip through the atmosphere and reach the earth's surface are called meteorites.

Some meteoroids are tiny—smaller than specks of dust. They give off heat very quickly and neither glow nor burn up. Instead, they simply drift down through the atmosphere. Tons of these meteorites reach the earth's surface every day and mingle with ordinary dust.

Other meteorites are chunks of rock, metal, or rock and metal. They are the remains of fireballs, like the one over Weston in 1807. Fireballs often explode, and their pieces rain down over several square miles.

Before the meteorite hit the Donahues' house, a fireball lighted up thousands of square miles in New York State and southern New England. Police stations were flooded with calls reporting bright lights in the sky and then an explosion. One observer saw the meteor break into three bright points of light. Most of it burned up in the atmosphere, but some pieces may have fallen unseen to earth—and one piece came to rest under a dining-room table.

That rock belonged to the Donahues, but they lent it to scientists who wanted to study it. As voyagers from space, meteorites are major clues to the history of our planet. From them, scientists learn about the birth of the solar system and the shaping of the planets.

The Donahues' meteorite turned out to be a kind of rock that is the oldest known, a kind that dates back to the time 4.6 billion years ago when the solar system was just forming.

2.

Ancient Collisions

BILLIONS of years ago, a vast cloud of gas and dust was floating in space and slowly rotating. Then for some reason the cloud began to collapse, drawing in on itself. Becoming smaller, the cloud became more dense—the gas and dust in it were packed more closely together.

As the cloud went on drawing in, it rotated faster and flattened into a disk. For millions of years, gas and dust kept spiraling into the center of the disk, creating pressure that caused the center to become hotter and hotter. Finally the heat and pressure became so great that atoms began to fuse, making the center glow with nuclear fires. In this

The Crab Nebula is the remains of a star that exploded. Shock waves from a similar explosion may have triggered the collapse of the cloud of gas and dust that became our solar system.

way, many astronomers think, a new star was born. It was the one we call our sun.

The planets were probably born of collisions in the surrounding disk of gas and dust. The first collisions were among dust particles, which stuck together the way big snowflakes do, forming clumps. Clumps collided with clumps. Larger clumps swept up smaller ones. As the clumps gained mass, their gravitational force increased. They drew more and more matter to themselves and grew bigger and bigger. In this way planets took shape. After perhaps a hundred million years, a family of young planets was orbiting the young sun. There were the four small, inner planets we call Mercury, Venus, Earth, and Mars, and the four giant, outer planets we call Jupiter, Saturn, Uranus, and Neptune. (Astronomers are not sure when tiny Pluto formed.) Of all the planets, Jupiter apparently formed fastest, pulling to itself so much material that it became the giant of them all.

Between Mars and Jupiter was a belt of rocks—the asteroids—some small, some large, each in orbit around the sun. Asteroids may be the material of a planet that never took shape, that perhaps could not because the gravitation of giant Jupiter kept the pieces from coming together.

The Orion Nebula is a place where hundreds of stars—and perhaps planets—are being born. The clouds of gas and dust are lighted from within by the glow of newborn stars.

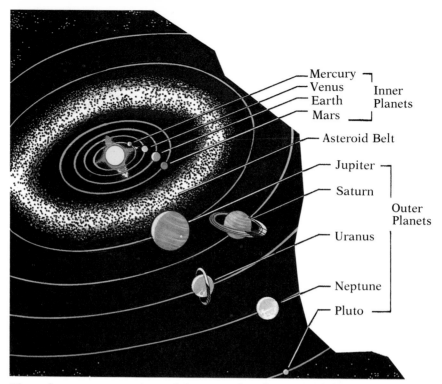

Mercury ⎤
Venus   ⎥ Inner
Earth   ⎥ Planets
Mars ____⎦

— Asteroid Belt

— Jupiter ⎤
— Saturn ⎥
          ⎥ Outer
          ⎥ Planets
— Uranus ⎥
— Neptune ⎥
— Pluto __⎦

The solar system consists of the sun, the planets and their moons, as-
teroids, and a huge cloud of comets that is too far away to show here.
The planets appear larger than if drawn to scale.

In the frigid outer reaches of the solar system, far from the sun's warming rays, were billions upon billions of comets. Formed of ices and dust particles, they were like big, dirty snowballs, half a mile or more in diameter.

When the inner planets were young, they were so hot that they were molten. Heavier elements, such as iron, settled toward the center of the planets, forming a core in each. The core was surrounded by layers of less dense rock. As the planets cooled, they developed solid crusts.

The solar system was full of comets and mountain-sized rocks left over from the formation of the planets.

These were hurtling through space at speeds of 20,000 to 50,000 miles an hour. When they crashed into rocky planets, they gouged out huge craters. Sometimes they broke through crust, releasing floods of molten rock. Many astronomers think that Earth's moon formed at this time, when an object the size of Mars struck our planet a glancing blow. The collision crushed and vaporized both the object's crust and Earth's. Molten material squirted outward in a huge jet, then spread into a disk. Within the disk, particles collided with particles, and tiny moons formed. They collided, making bigger moons, and within

Satellite studies indicate that the very bright star Vega is surrounded by a cloud of cold, dusty particles, left over from its birth. The cloud is shown here in an artist's painting.

Craters on the face of Jupiter's moon Callisto tell of a time when planets and moons were battered by collisions with comets and hurtling chunks of rock, some the size of mountains.

a few hundred years our moon took shape. Meanwhile, the earth had re-formed, combining its own material with most of the material of the colliding object.

Among the outer planets, comets slammed into moons. They collided with giant planets and disappeared into the deep atmospheres. Still other comets were hurled about by the strong gravitation of Jupiter and Saturn. Many were flung, like stones from a slingshot, far out into space. They became part of the huge cloud of comets that still orbit the sun on the outer edges of the solar system.

After several hundred million years the violence grew less. Many of the hurtling rocks and comets had been used up.

On Earth the scars of that ancient bombardment have disappeared, for the earth is an active planet, a planet of change. Because the earth has an atmosphere, it has weather. Weathering wears down rock and alters the face

The cratered face of Mercury also bears silent witness to the ancient bombardment of giant rocks and comets.

of the earth. On our changing planet, old mountains wear away and new ones crumple out of the crust. Volcanoes erupt. Ocean levels change. New crust forms, and old crust is destroyed.

When we look out into the solar system, however, we see the scars on other planets and on moons. The face of Earth's moon, for example, is pocked with craters, some the size of Texas. They have changed very little, because the moon has no atmosphere. Its gravity is too weak to hold one. Without an atmosphere, the moon has no weather and no weathering of rock. Its face tells of a time when the moon was still so hot inside that molten rock welled up, spread across the surface, and flowed into craters. It tells of the many years when the moon was being battered by giant rocks.

Scientists are able to date ancient bombardments through rocks that were once molten—lava flows and rock that melted in the heat of collisions. These rocks hold tiny amounts of elements that are radioactive. That is, the elements decay—they break down and give off parts of themselves.

Because they are giving off parts of themselves, the atoms of these elements are changed. They become atoms of another element. For example, there is a form of potassium called potassium 40. When its atoms break down,

Volcanoes, pouring out floods of lava, are one sign of an active planet, where ancient scars are often hidden or erased.

they form atoms of argon. Scientists know the rate at which potassium 40 breaks down. Over 8.4 billion years, one half of its atoms will decay into atoms of argon. Over the next 8.4 billion years, half the remaining atoms of potassium 40 will decay into argon, and so on. By measuring the number of potassium atoms and the number of argon atoms in a rock sample, scientists can work out the age of the rock.

Rock samples from the moon have enabled scientists to date ancient collisions in the solar system.

This moon rock, brought back by Apollo 12 astronauts, was found to be about 4 billion years old.

In other words, radioactive elements serve as clocks. As soon as molten rock hardens, the clock starts to run.

When the Apollo astronauts brought back rocks from the moon, scientists were able to date these samples. Rock that hardened after large craters had been blasted out of the moon proved to be 3.8 to 4.6 billion years old. The dating of these and other moon rocks seems to show that the heavy bombardment ended about 3.8 billion years ago.

What happened to the moon must have happened to the earth and other planets, and so the moon rocks have helped to establish a timetable for events in the young solar system. They have added to knowledge gained by studying other ancient rocks—meteorites, most of which seem to have come from asteroids.

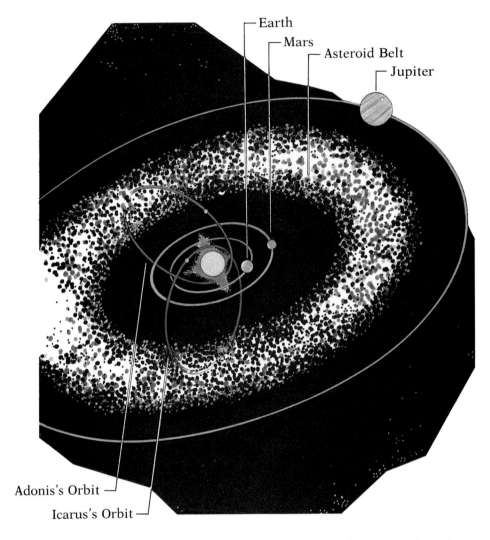

Most of the asteroids lie in a belt between Mars and Jupiter. Others share Jupiter's orbit. And a few, such as Adonis and Icarus, have orbits that cross the earth's orbit.

3.

Asteroids: *In Space, on Earth*

COMPARED with planets, asteroids are small. The largest is 600 miles in diameter, while the smallest measure only a mile or two across. If all the tens of thousands of them could be put together, they would not make a planet as big as our moon.

Far and away the largest number of asteroids orbit the sun in the belt of space between Mars and Jupiter. Dozens of others, called Trojans, share the orbit of Jupiter. Another group, the Apollo asteroids, have orbits that cross the earth's. So far, about thirty of these have been observed. Most measure a mile or more across. Scientists suspect there are thousands of other Apollos too small to be seen from Earth.

No asteroid is big enough or close enough to Earth

to be seen without a telescope. With a telescope, asteroids appear only as points of light, blurred by the earth's atmosphere. Yet scientists have learned a good deal about them.

Radar echoes show that asteroids may be shaped like bricks, potatoes, and barbells. Some appear to be clumps of four or five mountain-sized rocks stuck together. Some travel in groups.

Other studies tell how big asteroids are and how rough

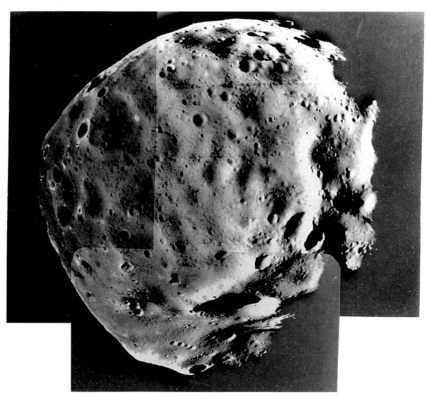

From Earth, asteroids appear only as blurry points of light. Phobos (above), the larger moon of Mars, . . .

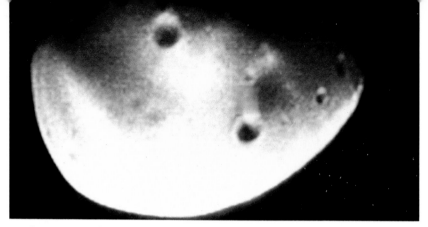

and Deimos (above), the smaller, may be asteroids that Mars captured. If so, these photos taken by Viking Orbiter 1 show us what asteroids look like.

and dark their surfaces are. Most important, scientists have learned what asteroids are made of by analyzing the light reflected from them. Many are made of the same materials as meteorites. And so it seems that most meteorites were asteroids for billions of years before they fell to earth.

There are three big, broad groups of meteorites.

One group is known as the irons, although these meteorites may also contain nickel. Only about 5 percent of the meteorites that strike the earth are irons, but irons are by far the easiest to find. They do not look like ordinary rocks, they stick to magnets, and they trigger metal detectors. The largest known meteorite is an iron, which lies on a farm in Namibia, in southwest Africa. It weighs some seventy tons. The irons seem to show that long ago there were some very large asteroids that had formed iron cores, just as planets did. Collisions broke up the asteroids, and some of the cores later became meteorites.

The Cape York, a huge iron meteorite weighing 68,085 pounds, was found in Greenland and brought to New York City in 1896. It is on display at the American Museum of Natural History.

The second group of meteorites is called stony-irons. These are a mixture of rock and iron metal. Less than 2 percent of all known meteorites are stony-irons.

The third group is the stony meteorites, or stones. They are made mostly of rocky material. More than 90 percent of the meteorites that strike the earth are stones, but they are hard to find unless they're seen to fall. After they have weathered a little, they look just like ordinary rocks.

The best hunting ground for meteorites has turned out to be Antarctica. Meteorites that fall there are covered by deep snows that pack down into ice. The ice is so thick that it flows, under the pressure of its own weight. Meteorites buried in the ice are carried along. Much of the ice flows to the sea, where tongues of it break off and float away as icebergs. Any meteorites in that ice are lost when the bergs melt. But there are places where the flow of ice is stopped by a mountain barrier. The ice pushes up against the barrier, bringing its cargo of meteorites near the surface. Wind wears away ice and snow, exposing the meteorites. During the brief antarctic summer, they can be seen from a low-flying helicopter, lying on the ice like a windfall of apples.

These meteorites were first discovered in 1968. Within ten years, scientists had collected more than 6,000 meteorite samples, pieces of perhaps 600 meteorites that had fallen over thousands and thousands of years. In the previous 200 years, scientists had found only 2,400 meteorite samples. None of these had been on Earth for more than 200 to 300 years. Laboratory tests show that most of the antarctic meteorites fell 30,000 to 400,000 years ago, and at least one has been here for 700,000 years.

Many of the antarctic finds are the stony meteorites known as chondrites. Their name comes from the small, rounded bodies called chondrules that are scattered through them. Because chondrules have never been found in any Earth rocks, they were long a mystery. Today scientists think that chondrites are the oldest rocks in the solar system and that chondrules formed from droplets of molten rock in the spinning disk that gave rise to the solar system.

Ordinary chondrites are common kinds of meteorites—it was an ordinary chondrite that crashed through the roof of the Donahues' house in Wethersfield. But certain other stony meteorites found in Antarctica are anything but common.

Chondrites are named for the tiny bodies called chondrules in them. They may be the oldest rocks in the solar system.

Some seem to be pieces of the moon. They are unlike any Earth rocks or any other known meteorites. But they are very much like rocks that the astronauts brought back from the moon. So far, four of these meteorites have been found. Studies show that two of them once formed a single larger piece that broke apart.

Two other antarctic meteorites belong to a small group known as SNCs (pronounced "snicks"). The name comes from the initials of places where three SNCs were seen to fall: Shergotty (India), Nakhla (Egypt), and Chassigny (France). The antarctic finds brought the total number of known SNCs to eight.

SNCs contain glassy material that is formed by shock waves, probably caused by a powerful collision. And all are much younger than other meteorites. Most meteorites are 4.5 billion years old. The SNCs are about 1.3 billion.

The age of the SNCs is a clue to where they came from. Their parent body must be a place where volcanic eruptions were taking place 1.3 billion years ago—where molten rock hardened, and atomic clocks began to run. The most likely place seems to be Mars. That planet has several huge volcanoes that may have been active 1.3 billion years ago. And in addition, its craters show that Mars has been struck by many large meteoroids.

The two Viking Lander probes that touched down on Mars in 1976 sent back information about the martian soil and atmosphere. The same gases that make up the

Two antarctic meteorites: Above, a rock from Mars, 1.3 billion years old. Below, a moon rock, perhaps from the far side.

atmosphere appear in a SNC from Antarctica. The chemical elements that make up the soil of Mars are a close match for those of the Shergotty meteorite.

At first, though, it was not clear how rocks could travel from Mars to Earth. To escape from Mars a rock would need a velocity of three miles a second. It would take a powerful collision indeed to accelerate rocks to that speed. And early experiments showed that such a collision would grind the rocks to powder, melt them, or turn them to vapor. But now scientists working with new experiments and computers think they have solved the problem. Suppose, they say, a meteoroid one tenth of a mile in diameter was traveling at 16,000 miles an hour and hit Mars at an angle. It would instantly vaporize enough of itself and Mars to produce a blast of hot gas. Jets of gas traveling at 50,000 miles an hour could accelerate rocks to a speed of 11,300 miles an hour, a speed great enough for them to escape Mars. And so it seems that at least some SNCs are indeed pieces of Mars.

The objects that collided with Mars may have been asteroids. They may equally well have been another kind of space voyagers—comets.

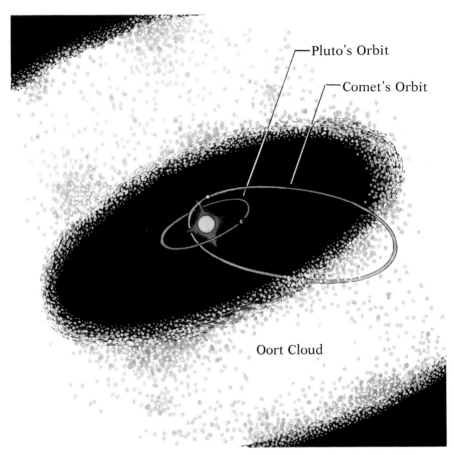

Pluto's Orbit

Comet's Orbit

Oort Cloud

Comets nudged out of the Oort cloud plunge inward, loop around the sun, and head out again. Both coming and going, they cut across the orbits of planets. Diagram is not to scale—if Pluto's orbit were made the size of a dime, comets in the cloud would have to be about 30 feet away.

4.

Comets: *Visitors from Outer Space*

FAR out in space, beyond the most distant planets, is a vast cloud of comets that circle the sun at speeds of about 200 miles an hour. It is called the Oort cloud, after a Dutch astronomer who first showed that it must exist. There are billions upon billions of these comets. In the deep freeze of outer space, they are chunks of ice—frozen water and frozen gases—mixed with dust and perhaps rocks.

From time to time, comets leave their distant orbits, perhaps because they were nudged by the gravity of passing stars. These stars, like our sun, are part of the large group called the Milky Way Galaxy. All the stars in the Galaxy are in motion. And so it happens that other stars sometimes pass by our solar system, although at a great distance away. Comets might also be disturbed at times

Halley's Comet was a brilliant spectacle when it passed the earth in 1910. The original of this photograph was processed by a computer, with colors added to show levels of brightness.

when the solar system plows through one of the huge clouds of gas and dust in space.

When comets are nudged out of their orbits, some are lost in space. Others take up new orbits, which have the shape of a flattened circle, or ellipse. Such a comet plunges toward the sun, loops around it, and returns to space, only to start a new plunge toward the sun.

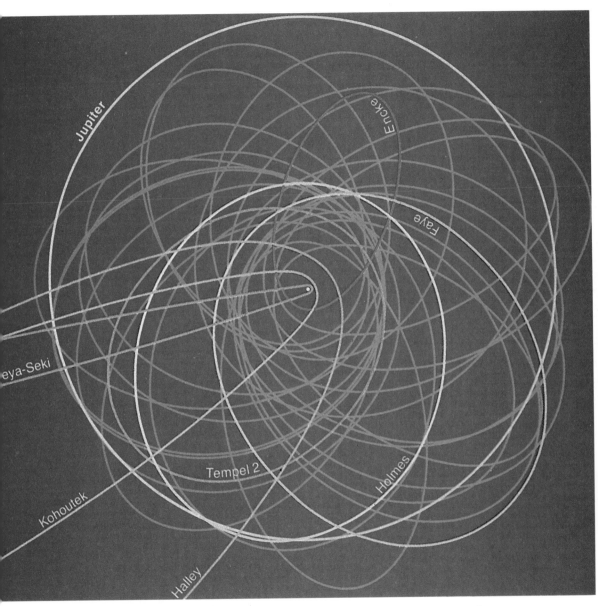

A few of the known comet orbits are shown here in relation to Jupiter's orbit. Many of these comets were affected by the gravitational pull of a planet and put into small orbits.

In its new orbit, a comet crosses the orbits of planets. Sometimes a planet is nearby at the time of the crossing, and its gravitational pull affects the course of the comet.

Shortly after this photograph was taken in 1965, Comet Ikeya-Seki passed so close to the sun that the sun's gravitational tug caused the comet to split in two.

The comet may be put into a smaller orbit. It no longer travels far out beyond Pluto but stays in the same part of the solar system as the planets.

When a comet nears the inner planets, it begins to be warmed by the sun. Its outer ices change to gases. Gases and dust from the comet spread out around the solid core for tens or hundreds of thousands of miles, forming an atmosphere, or head. The sun's rays make the gases glow. If the comet can be seen in our night sky, it looks like a fuzzy ball of light. It does not streak across the sky like a meteor but rises and sets with the stars.

As the comet moves closer to the sun, another change takes place. Light and other radiation from the sun act on the comet's head. They force dust and gases back from the head into a tail, or sometimes into more than one tail. A tail may stretch out for 100 million miles or more.

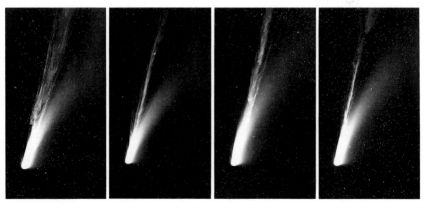

Comet Mrkos was photographed for four nights: August 22, 24, 25, and 27, 1957. It proved to be one of the comets that develop two tails. Some comets develop more than two.

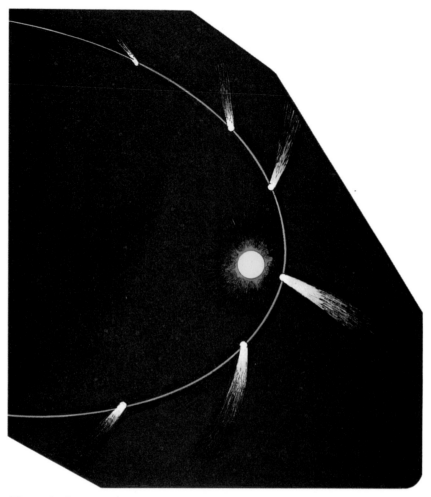

The tail of a comet always points away from the sun, no matter whether the comet is approaching or moving away from the sun.

It always points away from the sun. When a comet is approaching the sun, the tail stretches out behind it or to one side. When a comet moves away from the sun, the tail goes first. Once a comet leaves the warming rays of the sun behind, it stops giving off gases and dust.

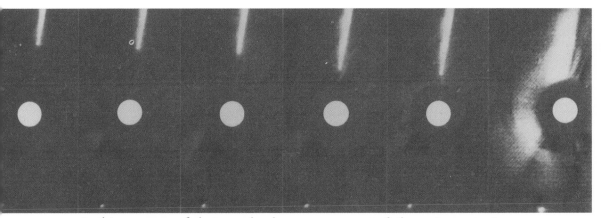

As this sequence of photographs shows, some comets fail to swing around the sun. On August 30, 1979, Comet Howard-Koomen-Michels plunged into the sun and was destroyed.

When Halley's Comet approached the sun in 1986, space probes sent back photographs that gave scientists their first close look at a comet. Fiery clouds of gas and dust and a jumble of icy boulders surrounded the core. The core itself was the shape of a baking potato ten miles long and five miles wide—much larger than scientists had expected—and blacker than coal. The blackness was caused by dust embedded in the ice. This coating of dust had built up on the core during earlier swings around the sun, when ice and dust changed to gases and dust. Gases escaped and dust was left.

There were spots on the surface of the core where high-powered jets of gas and dust from inside erupted like geysers. Scientists estimated that Halley's Comet was shedding at least forty tons of matter a second through those jets.

Halley's Comet was most recently seen in 1986. It is now traveling toward the far end of its orbit, beyond Neptune.

Any comet that passes near the sun loses gases and dust, and never recaptures them. The gases drift off into space. The lost dust gradually fills the space around the comet's orbit. The result is something like a stretched-out doughnut. When the earth, traveling in its own orbit, passes through part of a dust doughnut, the larger particles plunge into the atmosphere and burn up. We see these brilliant streaks of light as a shower of meteors. The smaller particles drift slowly down through the atmosphere. We meet them as dust.

Meteor showers form in the earth's atmosphere, but they look as if they were coming from constellations and are named for them. The Perseid shower, for example,

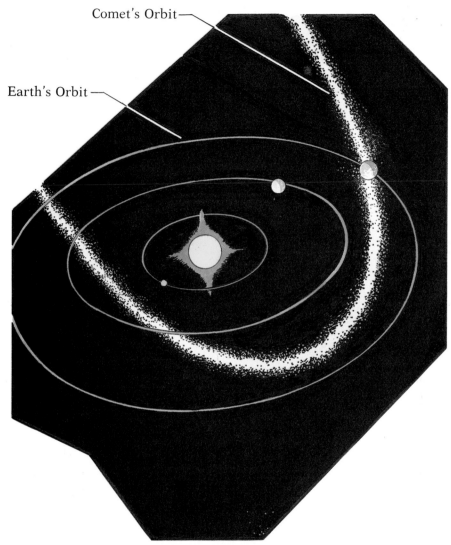

Comet's Orbit

Earth's Orbit

Meteor showers occur when the earth passes through the stream of dust particles shed by a comet and left behind in the comet's orbit.

appears around August 12 each year and seems to be coming from the constellation Perseus. The Geminids, which occur around December 14, seem to be coming from Gemini.

Small comets that lose their gases probably lose all their solid matter as well. The comet disappears, and only a stretched-out doughnut of dust is left—the stuff of meteors. Something different may happen with large comets. A large comet might have a rocky core and lose all its other material. Or it might have sizable chunks of rock in it, rocks too big to be blown off by the gases. In time the rocks might come to cover the comet's surface. The comet would go on orbiting the sun, but it would no longer give off gases that formed an atmosphere or tail. The same thing might happen if a comet built up a thick coating of dust.

A comet stripped down to a rocky core or a comet with an overcoat of dust or rock would look like an asteroid.

For a number of years astronomers suspected that certain asteroids were really former comets. They thought some of the asteroids that cross the orbits of Earth and other planets might really be the remains of comets. So might some other asteroids with cometlike orbits.

Then in 1983 the Infrared Astronomy Satellite, called IRAS, discovered a small, dark object that showed no trace of an atmosphere or a tail. Identified as 1983 TB, it at first appeared to be an Apollo asteroid. But studies showed that its orbit had the shape of an ellipse and that it traveled closer to the sun than any other Apollo. Most important, 1983 TB was traveling in the same orbit as the dust particles that cause the Geminid meteor shower. It is unlikely that an asteroid would somehow come to share this orbit. It is much more likely that 1983 TB is the remains of the comet that shed the dust particles. If so, this explains why astronomers had never been able to find the comet that was the source of the Geminids: It had taken on the appearance of an asteroid and orbited unseen until IRAS found it.

Once, it seemed easy to tell a comet from an asteroid. Today astronomers are learning that some small, dark objects that look like asteroids are really former comets. There may even be former comets in the asteroid belt. Astronomers are also learning that comets may have played a part in shaping planets, including Earth.

Voyager 2 looked back at this sunlit crescent of Uranus. The planet appears blue-green because of methane in the atmosphere.

5.

Comets and Planets

FOR years many astronomers thought that the four giant planets had all formed in the same way, by gathering up gases and dust from the spinning disk. Studying light reflected from the planets, they identified the gases in each atmosphere. These studies showed that Jupiter and Saturn were closely related. Uranus and Neptune, however, seemed more closely related to comets than to their big neighbors. Some astronomers wondered if comets were leftovers, if they had formed from gases and dust that were not swept up by Uranus and Neptune.

Other astronomers had a different idea. Perhaps, they said, as the sun and inner planets were forming, only Jupiter and Saturn took shape. Beyond Saturn there were no planets, only billions and billions of comets, traveling around the sun near the present orbits of Uranus and Neptune. Comets kept colliding and sticking together, and in this way two big planets formed. Comets that were not used up were flung out of their orbits and became the Oort cloud.

At the time this idea was suggested, there was no way to prove it right or wrong. But now there is evidence that it may be right. The evidence comes from observations made by Voyager 2, which sailed past Uranus in early 1986.

As expected, Uranus proved to have a rocky core, about the size of Earth. The core, scientists now think, is wrapped in a dense and icy atmosphere of water, methane, and ammonia, topped by a thin layer of hydrogen mixed with a little helium and neon. The ices in comets are also made mostly of water, methane, and ammonia, but the atmospheres of Jupiter and Saturn are chiefly hydrogen and helium. And so there is reason to think that Uranus is closely related to comets. It may well have formed, wholly or partly, out of colliding comets.

Astronomers also used to think that nearly all comets were in the far reaches of the solar system. Now they suspect that a great many comets may be traveling unseen among the inner planets. They think that from time to time a passing star comes close enough to the Oort cloud to scatter a billion comets at once and shower the inner solar system with them over a period of a million years.

Unless they are near the sun, comets are small and dark and almost impossible to detect from Earth. But in a nine-month period, when it was searching for asteroids, IRAS discovered five comets in the inner solar system and hints of many more.

Scientists have long known that comets must have battered the young Earth. Some have thought that melted comets may have formed pools that became the first oceans. Water was added to the pools when volcanic eruptions released water vapor that condensed and fell as rain.

A new theory suggests that comets may still be supplying the earth with water, that small, icy comets keep hurtling into the earth's upper atmosphere, breaking up, and releasing water vapor. The water, falling as rain, is added to Earth's own water.

The new theory grew out of some puzzling observations made by a team of scientists who were working with a space satellite. It carried instruments designed to measure ultraviolet radiation being given off by the earth's atmosphere. Normally, images produced in this way make the earth look like a ball of gas. Half the ball is lighted by the sun, producing what is called dayglow. The other half is wrapped in darkness. When the scientists examined the images from the satellite, they kept finding little black spots or holes in the dayglow. The holes were usually thirty miles in diameter, and they formed and disappeared within three minutes.

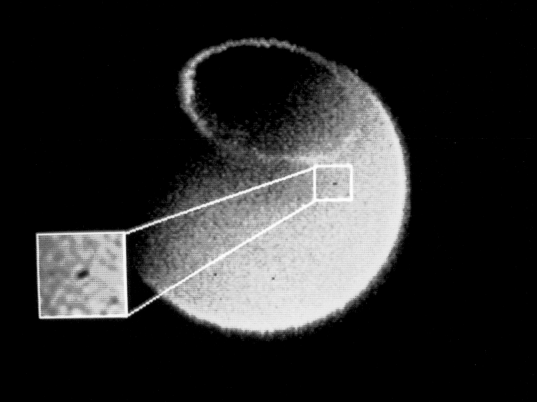

Images from a satellite show black spots or holes in the earth's dayglow. These may be caused by comets entering the atmosphere and changing to water vapor, which falls as rain.

At first the scientists thought something must have gone wrong with one of their instruments. Or perhaps flecks of paint from the satellite were making black spots on the images. But this was not the case. The holes were real. The team explored other possible explanations. Only one seemed to stand up: The black spots were being caused by clouds of water vapor some 180 miles above the earth. The clouds were blocking the ultraviolet radiation from view.

What was the source of the clouds of water vapor?

The most likely answer was small, icy comets, which were breaking up in the atmosphere and forming a large ball of water vapor or fluffy snow.

To account for the size of the black spots, each comet-caused cloud would have to contain about a hundred tons of water. This is not very much, not even enough to cause a heavy rain. But the spots were forming at a rate of twenty a minute. So if each black spot is really a hundred tons of water, and if comets have been arriving for billions of years, then the earth has received a truly enormous amount of water.

Scientists are just starting to discover the part that comets, past and present, have played in the earth's history. This comet is Kohoutek, which arrived from the Oort cloud in 1973.

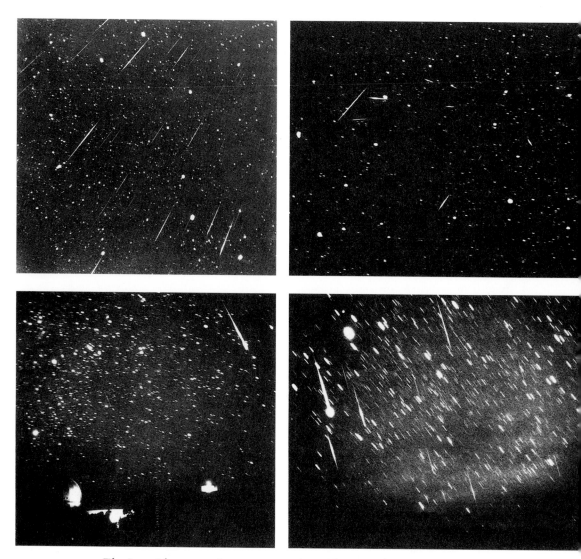

The Leonid meteor shower occurs in mid-November and is one of several showers that take place regularly. The blurring of the stars is caused by Earth's rotation while the camera shutter was open.

Showers of comets—if they really occur—might do more than supply water. Perhaps there are times when the number of arriving comets increases sharply. The added water vapor forms a cloud layer and reduces the amount of sunlight reaching Earth's surface. The result might be an ice age, a time when more snow falls in winter than the summer sun can melt, and glaciers grow for thousands of years. Or if a great deal of sunlight was cut off, plants might die and animals would lose their food source. Such a change could explain what happened to the dinosaurs and many other forms of life that died out at the same time.

So far the theory is no more than a theory. No one has ever seen one of the small, icy comets. No other scientists have detected black spots in the dayglow. Until others have a chance to test the team's findings, there is no way to tell if the theory is true.

At the same time, however, there is no doubt that voyagers from space have sometimes had a big effect on the earth.

Charred and flattened trees mark the Tunguska region of Siberia, where a fiery object, thought to have been part of a comet, exploded violently on June 30, 1908.

6.

The Tunguska Event

AT 7:17 on the morning of June 30, 1908, something fell out of the sky over northern Asia, exploded at an altitude of five miles, and knocked down a forest in the Tunguska region of Siberia.

Some forty miles away from the center of the blast, a farmer was sitting on the steps of the trading post when the whole northern part of the sky appeared to catch fire. He heard a bang and a crash. The shock waves knocked him unconscious.

Still another farmer told of "a long flaming object flying through the sky. It was many times bigger than the sun but much dimmer. . . . Behind the flames trailed what looked like dust. It was wreathed in little puffs, and blue streamers were left behind from the flames." This farmer also heard great blasts and felt the ground tremble. The windowpanes in his cabin were shattered.

The witnesses were lucky to be miles away from the center of the blast. Directly beneath it, 800,000 acres of forest burst into flame. Farther away, in a region covering hundreds of square miles, trees toppled, their trunks pointing outward from the blast, like spokes of a wheel. During the next few nights the sky was bright over parts of Europe and western Asia. The cause was dust from the explosion, drifting through the atmosphere and reflecting light from a sun that was below the horizon.

The explosion was the most powerful ever recorded. Yet the cause of the Tunguska Event, as it is called, remains a mystery. Scientists are sure the exploding object was either an asteroid or part of a comet, but they cannot tell which. The Tunguska object made no crater and left no telltale pieces of itself. If the object was an asteroid, it must have shattered into dust, which drifted down and mixed with other dust on Earth. If it was a comet, its ice must have turned to water or vapor, while its dust drifted earthward.

One recent theory proposes that the Tunguska object was part of a comet that broke up at least 1,500 years ago, leaving a swarm of about 100 large fragments orbiting the sun. One of the fragments is what we call Comet Encke. Still other giant chunks of ice are spread out over a region 10 million miles long. The rest of the orbit holds dust.

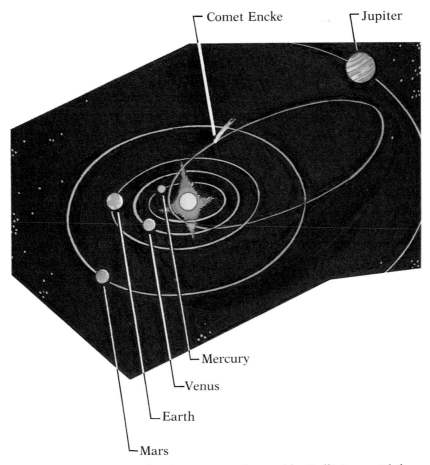

- Comet Encke
- Jupiter
- Mercury
- Venus
- Earth
- Mars

Comet Encke has an orbit that crosses the earth's. Collisions with large chunks of matter in that orbit may explain certain mysterious events on the earth and on its moon.

The orbit crosses the orbit of the earth. Most of the time Earth meets only dust particles when it passes through. These are probably the source of the Taurid meteor showers, which we see in June and November. But sometimes Earth and its moon meet larger fragments, according to the scientist who developed this theory. He has calculated the dates on which the earth and the moon may have passed through the swarm of large fragments. If he is right, the Tunguska Event is one of several strange happenings that might be explained.

An early one took place on June 25, 1178, and was observed by monks in Canterbury, England. They recorded that when the moon was a thin crescent, "The upper horn of the new moon seemed to split in two and a flame shot from it."

A recent one took place from June 22 to 26, 1975, when the moon was shaken by the strongest bombardment of meteoroids ever recorded.

The first chance to test the theory will come in the year 2042. If the swarm of large fragments really exists, that is when the earth and moon will next pass through them.

The Tunguska object left only one clue to itself. Scientists have found tiny particles on the ground that contain a chemical element called iridium.

Earth has iridium, but most of it is in the core. Iridium tends to move with iron, and at the time when the earth was molten, most of the iron settled toward the center of our planet.

Meteorites are richer in iridium than the earth's crust is. So when scientists find unusual amounts of iridium on Earth, they can be fairly sure that it came from a meteorite. The tiny particles from Tunguska held just such a clue.

Other studies showed traces of the Tunguska explosion as far away as Antarctica. There yearly snowfalls pack down into layers of ice. When a core is taken from the ice, the layers can be seen, like so many tree rings. They can be dated backward from the most recent, or top, layers.

Antarctic ice that formed from the snows of 1908 was four times richer in iridium than the ice of earlier years. During 1909 and the next few years, the snows were also rich in iridium. These findings show that particles from the shattered object were carried by winds around the world for several years. As the particles settled out of the air or fell in rain and snow, the Tunguska Event left its traces far from Siberia.

Unusual amounts of iridium were also laid down 65 million years ago. They tell of a collision that may have brought about the end of the dinosaurs.

Although dinosaurs died out long before there were people to tell of them, we know about them through their fossils.

7.

Dinosaurs and Meteorites

FROM time to time in Earth's long history, far-reaching changes have taken place. As a result, large numbers of many kinds of plants and animals have died out completely, never to be seen again. Such a dying out is called a mass extinction.

The clues to mass extinctions are fossils—the remains and traces of ancient animals and plants that have been preserved in layers of rock. Fossils tell of many forms of life that flourished for millions of years. Then something happened, and they died out, or became extinct. Because scientists are able to date the layers of rock, they can tell when the plants and animals lived and when they died out.

The fossil record shows a number of periods in Earth's history when mass extinctions took place. The most famous happened about 65 million years ago, when the dinosaurs died out. At that same time, many other large groups of plants and animals also became extinct, both on land and in the sea. They disappear from the fossil record along with the dinosaurs.

What happened is one of the big mysteries of science. For years the most likely explanation seemed to be a change in climate. The fossil remains of plants show that for millions of years Earth's climate had been warm, and even tropical. By 65 million years ago, it had started to cool off. Many forms of life could no longer exist in the regions where they had been living. But a number of scientists felt this explanation was not good enough. They did not think that change of climate alone could account for the size of the mass extinction.

Now there is a new theory having to do with a meteorite. It grew from a chance discovery in a bed of limestone in Italy. The limestone had formed as tiny sea animals and plants died and their remains rained to the bottom of a shallow sea. The remains piled up and hardened into the kind of rock called limestone. From time to time the kinds of sea life changed. With each change, a different layer of rock formed. Millions of years ago, the shallow sea dried up, and the limestone became part of the land.

A thin layer of iridium-rich clay was discovered between two layers of limestone, marking a time of great change. (The coin, which is the size of a U.S. quarter, is used for scale.)

An American geologist, who was studying the limestone, made an odd discovery. He found a thin layer of clay sandwiched between two layers of limestone. The clay layer meant that at some time in the past a big change had taken place. Whatever it was had stopped the formation of limestone, had stopped the remains of sea life from raining down. Instead, tiny particles of clay had built up. Then the laying down of limestone began again.

Dating showed that the clay had been laid down 65 million years ago, the time when a major mass extinction had taken place. The clay also proved to be rich in iridium, so rich that the iridium seemed almost certain to have come from space.

With these discoveries, a new theory began to take shape. It suggests that a large meteorite, six to seven miles in diameter, struck the earth 65 million years ago. The collision sent vast quantities of material soaring into the atmosphere. As the material spread, it cut off sunlight and brought night to all parts of the earth. The darkness lasted for weeks, or even months. Without the sun's rays, temperatures dropped. Photosynthesis stopped, and green plants could no longer make their own food. Plants died on land and in the sea. Animals that ate plants died. So did animals that ate other animals. The survivors on land were mostly seeds, roots, and bulbs, and small animals, especially those that burrowed.

Gradually the atmosphere cleared, as dust settled out of it and laid down a layer of iridium-rich clay. The sun's rays once more reached the earth. By then, on land and in the sea, many forms of life had become extinct. Among them were the dinosaurs and the tiny sea creatures and plants whose remains had built the limestone now in Italy. In time, new and different layers of limestone were laid down on top of the iridium-rich clay by the remains of other small forms of sea life.

The new theory stirred great interest and debate. Scientists who had been working with fossils argued that the new theory was wrong. Their studies suggested that the dinosaurs had died out over a long period of time, as the earth itself slowly changed.

Later, many of these scientists changed their minds, at least a bit, as new evidence was found in layers of rock known to be 65 million years old. In sixty far-flung places, the same iridium-rich layer of clay was found. The most likely explanation of the clay is a great collision between the earth and a meteorite.

In studying iridium-rich clay samples from Denmark, Spain, and New Zealand, one team of scientists found that these all held soot. They think that if a great collision did take place, the heat created must have set off gigantic fires, far bigger than any we have ever known. Winds then carried smoke and soot around the world. The soot settled out, along with the dust that formed the clay layer. If this idea is right, then in some places the long dark night was accompanied by the soaring flames of rapidly spreading wildfire.

The mass extinction of 65 million years ago is one of several in Earth's long history. The fossil record shows at least six major mass extinctions in the past 600 million years, as well as a number of small ones. Are there signs that these might have been caused by collisions with meteorites? Teams of scientists have been trying to find out.

These tektites, shown magnified to about 50 times their true size, are so small that they are known as microtektites. They formed 700,000 years ago, probably during a big collision.

Some have searched for iridium in layers of rock that formed at the time of other mass extinctions.

Some have looked for other signs of great collisions. They are, for example, studying tektites, which are strange, small, glassy objects unlike any other glass known on Earth. Tektites come from materials found on Earth and changed by heat to a glassy form. They also contain iridium. They seem to be a product of big collisions, when material from the earth and a meteorite mixed, was heated, and blasted into the air. Millions of tons of tektites shot off and in some cases were strewn over areas a thousand miles long.

Many tektites have been found on land, and in a few cases the crater they came from is known. Great numbers of very small tektites have also been found buried in the ocean floors.

Tektites can be dated, and so they, too, are clues to when ancient collisions took place.

Other clues are found in big craters. Because the face of the earth is constantly changing, many ancient craters have been destroyed. But about a hundred large craters are known, most of them recently discovered with the help of satellite photographs. Craters, too, can be dated.

Some scientists have screened the fossil record, trying to date all mass extinctions, both large and small.

In putting all the clues together, a few teams of scientists think they have found a pattern. They think that large meteorites strike the earth on a regular basis, causing mass extinctions. One group thinks this happens every 26 to 28 million years, another that it happens every 33 million years. If so, then the meteorites are probably comets, not asteroids. As far as anyone knows, collisions with asteroids happen at random. There is no pattern.

What might disturb comets on a regular basis? What might nudge them into new orbits and put some on a collision course with the earth? There are several possibilities.

One involves Planet X. Astronomers have long wondered if there was an unseen tenth planet, Planet X, in the solar system, somewhere out beyond Pluto. If there is, its orbit might be such that every 28 million years Planet X sweeps through the inner edge of the Oort cloud. The result is a shower of comets, heading for the planets and sun.

Or perhaps the sun has a small dim companion star no one has ever seen. Such a star might pass near or through the Oort cloud from time to time, hurling some comets into space and sending others hurtling into the solar system. Most stars do have companions. Some have one, others more. Companion stars are bound together by gravitation and revolve around a central point. Like most stars, the sun may well have a companion, one so far unknown.

The problem with these and other ideas is that there is no way to test them. For example, Planet X may or may not exist. If it does, astronomers would have to find it and plot its orbit before they could say whether it might cause comet showers. The same thing is true of the companion star.

Someday, perhaps someday soon, we may know much more. We may learn if there is a pattern to Earth's collisions with comets—if millions of years from now there will be another great collision. We may learn what causes mass extinctions and what happened to the dinosaurs. But

Arizona's Meteor Crater formed about 50,000 years ago when an iron meteorite, traveling at 7 miles a second, slammed into the earth. The crater is 4,150 feet wide and 600 feet deep.

at present we know only what fossils tell us—that mass extinctions have taken place. We know only what craters and other evidence tell us—that from time to time the earth has collided with asteroids and comets.

We also know that voyagers from space will continue to cross Earth's orbit. These chunks of rock or ice are part of our solar system, and they have helped to make Earth

A near miss: On August 10, 1972, an object that was bigger than a diesel locomotive came in from space over Utah and sped north, disappearing over Canada. A vacationer at Jackson Lake, Wyoming, took this extraordinary photograph. His startled wife is looking up at what was probably an Apollo asteroid. The white streak was clearly visible, even in daylight.

into the planet we know. But with space satellites and other technology, we have the ability to protect ourselves. We could patrol space, discover any large object that is on a collision course with the earth, and change that course. And so the future may well be different from the past.

For Further Reading

Asimov, Isaac. *How Did We Find Out About Comets?* New York: Walker, 1975.

Branley, Franklyn M. *Halley: Comet 1986.* New York: Lodestar Books, 1983.

Couper, Heather. *Comets and Meteors.* New York: Franklin Watts, 1985.

Krupp, E. C. *The Comet and You.* New York: Macmillan, 1985.

Simon, Seymour. *The Long Journey from Space.* Crown, 1982.

Tillius, John. *The Science Digest Book of Halley's Comet.* New York: Avon, 1985.

Index

Numbers in *italics* refer to illustrations.

Photo Credits

Photographs in this book appear through the courtesy of:

cover: *(top on front cover; back cover)* Meteor crater in the Arizona desert — Francois Gohier/Photo Researchers, Inc. *(bottom left on front cover)* Galaxy through MMT telescope — Account Phototake/ Phototake NYC. *(bottom right on front cover)* Olvine-bronzite meteorite — University of Arizona/Account Phototake/Phototake NYC.

page vi: Dan Haar, *The Hartford Courant*

page 2: Battelle Pacific Northwest Laboratories

page 5: Yerkes Observatory

page 8: California Institute of Technology, © 1959

page 10: Photo by D. F. Malin. Copyright Anglo Australian Telescope Board, 1981

pages 13, 42: National Aeronautics and Space Administration (Jet Propulsion Laboratory)

pages 14, 15, 18, 22, 23: National Aeronautics and Space Administration

page 17: Photo by J. D. Griggs, United States Geological Survey, Hawaii Volcanoes National Park

pages 19, 28: National Aeronautics and Space Administration (Johnson Space Center)

page 24: Neg. #45085, Department of Library Services, American Museum of Natural History

page 26: Smithsonian Institution Photo No. M–1507B, Photo by Brian Mason

page 32: National Optical Astronomy Observatories and Lowell Observatory